Children's Letters to Socks

Kids Write to America's "First Cat"

Edited by

Bill Adler

A Birch Lane Press Book
Published by Carol Publishing Group

A Birch Lane Press Book
Published by Carol Publishing Group
Birch Lane Press is a registered trademark of Carol Communications, Inc.
Editorial Offices: 600 Madison Avenue, New York, N.Y. 10022
Sales and Distribution Offices: 120 Enterprise Avenue, Secaucus, N.J. 07094
In Canada: Canadian Manda Group, P.O. Box 920, Station U, Toronto, Ontario M8Z 5P9
Queries regarding rights and permissions should be addressed to
Carol Publishing Group, 600 Madison Avenue, New York, N.Y. 10022

Carol Publishing Group books are available at special discounts for bulk purchases,
sales promotions, fund raising, or educational purposes. Special editions can be
created to specifications. For details, contact Special Sales Department,
Carol Publishing Group, 120 Enterprise Avenue, Secaucus, N.J. 07094

Manufactured in the United States of America
10 9 8 7 6 5 4 3 2 1

Design by Steven Brower and Karen Coughlin

Library of Congress Cataloging-in-Publication Data
Children's Letters to Socks : kids write to America's "First Cat" /
      p.   cm.
   "A Birch Lane Press book."
   ISBN 1-55972-221-5
   1. Socks (Cat)—Humor. 2. Clinton, Bill, 1946-   —Humor.
   3. Presidents—United States—Pets—Humor.   4. Children—United States—
   Correspondence—Humor.   I. Adler, Bill.
   E887.C55C48   1994   93-46694
                                                                        0CIP

Dear socks:
I would like to send you a dead
mouse for your birthday?

From simon
age 8

DEAR SOCKS:
    MY CAT SAW YOU ON T.V.

HE SAID MEOW TO YOU BUT
YOU DIDN'T SAY MEOW BACK.

                YOUR FAN.
                MARK AGE 6
                PENNSAUKEN, N.J.

Dear Socks,

Do you ever meow at cabinet meetings?

Just curious,
Emily
Age 12
Houston

Dear Socks,
Our Cat Skipper always gets lost. You are lucky. If you get lost, the FBI will always find you.

Love,
Jessica
Age 11
Setauket, N.Y.

Dear Socks,
Do you have your own secret
service agent to guard you?

Rachael
Age 9
Setauket, N.Y.

11

Dear Socks:

I think the President should take you to his next press confrence.

Then when they ask the President nasty questions, he can change the subject and talk about you.

Your friend,
Eddie Lewis
age 9 Old Tappan N. J.

Dear Socks

Who chases mice in the White House.?
You or the F.B.I.

Sam
age 9

Dear Socks,
Is there a vet in the White House or do you have to see the presidents doctor when you are sick.

Sincerly
Murray
Age 10
Flushing

Dear Socks:

Please send me your autograph. If you can't do it, ask the president.

A friend,
Drew
Age 9
Houston, TX

Dear Socks

I think you have a cute face and i like your black and white paws.
I hope you have a lot of fun in the White House even if the president doesnt.

Love
Harry
age 5

Dear White House Cat

Please send me a picture of the white House mouse.

Love,
Jimmy H
Age 5
Waldwick

Dear socks:
Did you campaign with the President?
How many votes did you get?

Your fan,
kevin Lewis
age 8
old tappan

DEAR SOCKS.
DID YOU KNOW
MILLIE WHO
LIVED IN THE
WHITE
HOUSE WITH
PRESIDENT
BUSH?

LIA
AGE 5
HOUSTON

Dear saks:

I wondered if you could ask the President if he could try to help earth, mother nature, and animals. Because I love nature very, very much.

And can you see if he can help the endangered species.

Ideas,
make a very large zoo.
buy the land.
stop cutting down so many trees.
Think of more.

Your fan,
Jamma Brewer
Age 8
New Jersey

fox

socks

lapered

tiger? or not?

wolf

?

Danna Brower

Dear Socks:

Did you ever sleep on Lincoln's bed?

I once slept on a bed in a Holiday Inn.

Your fan,
Andrea K
Age 8.
New Jarsy

Socks

28

Dear Socks:
    I saw you on T.V. with
Dan Rather. Then I saw you on
Channel 4. You look better on
T.V. than the President.
                    Love,
                    Peter

Dear Socks,

you must get a lot of presents on Christmas! Is it fun in a house that big? I mean you can run around a lot! Your famous, you have your own stuffed animal too! I hope president Clinton gets to read this to you.

Love, Christina Romano

Dear Socks:

someday I am going to be President of the U.S.A.

When I am president of the U.S.A. I am going to have three dogs four cats six six tertles, 4 rabbits, a frog and five birds live with me in the White House.

Love,
James
Age 9
San Diego

Dear Socks:

You are the most famous cat in the U.S.A.

You should do a commercial for cat food.

Love Jonathan Suarez

Dear Socks,
I would like to come to the White House and play with you.

Any day is okay except Tuesday because I have to go to the dentist.

Love,
Bridget F.
Age 10
New Jersey

Bridget
Fitzgerald

Dear Socks,
I told my friend Melissa
that they gave you
a bath every day at
the White House
because they can't
have a dirty cat in
the White House.

Love
Katie
Age 10
MEDford

Socks

Dear Socks:
   Do you jog with the President?
You must be the fittest cat in
the U.S.A.

                    Your friend,
                    Larry

Dear Socks,

Did George Washington Have a cat? Please ask the Presidint if you don't Know the Answer.

Love Lara
age 9

Dear socks
I would like to ♥ Give you
a big kiss and Hug eveN if you
are a DemocRat. MY fatheR
████ doesN.t KNOW I WRote
this letter   Love Lisa ⬆ m 8

Dear Socks:

What will you do when you leave the White House? Maybe you could live with a movie star like Clint Eastwood.

A friend
Patrick 9,
San Francisco

Dear socks: do you
have any brothers
or sisters? my
brother lives with
us and it's

great!

xxx ooo Love
Rachel

TO SOCKS:
YOU should
be on the
Larry King
Show

Love
WilliAM

DEAR. SOCKS.
IS. YOUR. LITTER.
BOX. IN. THE. OVAL.

OFFICE? . A. FRIEND

SIMON

AGE. 5

. COLORADO

Dear Socks,
My cat Mickey, would like to
come and live with you in the
White House so he can be the
2nd cat.
              Love,
              Barney
              Age 8
              Brooklyn

Dear Socks,

Do you ever go to the Vet or does Mrs. Clinton have the Vet come to you? My cat, Louie, hates the Vet.

Your friend,
Betsy W

Dear Socks,

Do you have a girlfriend?

I'll bet any cat in the country would like to be your girl friend and live in the White House.

Love
Cathy R
Age 10
Milwaukee

Dear Socks:

My cat, Pretzal, would like to come and visit you at the White House.

Your friend,
Emily Earl
Age 10¾

P.S. Pretzel is a
Democrat

1600
Pennsylvania
Ave

Dear Socks,
How much do you weigh?
I hope you are not fat
like the president.

Love,
Jenny
age 8
Austin

56

Dear Cat in the White House,
Are you going to write the story of
your life when you leave the White
House like Millie did?

Your fan,
Lillian

Dear Socks,

I read that the President has his own chef. Does the chef cook for you too?

Sincerely,
Jessica Harrington

Jessica Harrington age 10

Dear socks;
When is your birthday?

I would like to send you a present
for your birthday that you can share
with the President, Mrs. Clinton and Chelsea.

your friend,
Karrin P,
Age 8

P.S I hope you like cheese cake

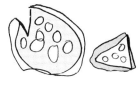

Dear First Cat:
    Do you know the first cat of any other country?

                    Love,
                    John F.
                    Age 8
                    N.J.

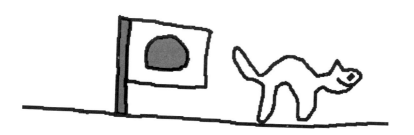

Dear Socks,

I have a cat named Harry and I play with Harry all the time.

I showed Harry a picture of you but he didn't say anything.

Your friend,
Randy B., age 10
Baltimore

Dear Socks,

I am saving my allowance so I can get a cat like you. It will take me 100 years.

Love,
Sebastian

Special Thanks To:

Mark Abbate, Harry Black, Sebastian Black, Simone Breunig Balog, Emily Breunig, Drew Breunig, Lia Breunig, Janna Brower, Sam Campodonico-Ludwig, Simon Campodonico-Ludwig, Lara Dolan, Lisa Dolan, Emily Earl, Bridget Fitzgerald, John Fitzgerald, Sarah Hamilton, Jessica Harrington, Jimmy Hascup, Jessica Landress, Rachael Landress, Eddie Lewis, Kevin Lewis, Karrin Pitt, Christina Romano, Rachel Schragis, William Schragis, Jonathan Suarez.